IRELAND

People and Landscape

Liam Blake's photographs offer an unsurpassed visual record of the beauties of Ireland and the day-to-day life of her people. His work over the years for the Real Ireland range of postcards has been a significant artistic achievement, influencing the perception of Ireland by the public and other photographers alike. His images in this book cover a wide-ranging spectrum of the Irish experience, ranging from small details of everyday life to sweeping panoramic landscapes. His vision and understanding of the Irish landscape and people provide the driving force for this book.

Book and Jacket Design by Brian Murphy.

Photography © Liam Blake.

Text David by Pritchard.

Published by Real Ireland Design
Picture House
16/17 Bullford Business Park,
Kilcoole, County Wicklow.

www.realireland.ie
info@realireland.ie

© Real Ireland Design 2014. This edition 2018.

A CIP catalogue record for this book is available from the British Library.

ISBN 0946887-323

Additional images supplied by camera Press for Beckett, Shaw and O'Casey; Yale University for Joyce;
G.A. Duncan for Behan; The Irish Times for Brian O'Nolan; Hulton Picture Library for Yeats; Patrick
Kavanagh © RTE Stills Library; The Board of Trinity College for Synge; The National Gallery For Swift
and Goldsmith.

Introduction

The name Ireland offers an insight into the place itself and its people. It is a derivation of the ancient Irish word Eire, which probably means Western. To its own people, then, Ireland was the country in the West, the last island before the vast Atlantic Ocean. The Greeks and Romans transliterated the same word into Ierne, or Ivernia, eventually calling the island Hibernia – the land of winter. This perhaps reflects one European view of Ireland, a cold wet remote island lost off the western edge of the world. Yet Ireland's isolation is illusory, for there has been a constant human interchange between her shores and those of her eastern neighbours for millennia. On this level the essence of the island has been woven into a unique cultural tapestry through the mingling of the diverse peoples who have contributed to its genius.

This book seeks to explore these seemingly contradictory visions of Ireland – as geographical dead-end or human crossroads. The first part charts the movement of the nameless folk who made their mark upon the landscape in Prehistory and at length emerged as the 'Irish', a distinct and recognizable People. The second looks at those remote western and northern coasts that face the wild ocean, the grandiose rim of the known world before the discovery of America and the cradle and deathbed of a Gaelic speaking society whose roots were found in the Stone Age. The last section covers the east of Ireland and Dublin, the gateway through which Viking, Norman and British colonists have influenced the historical evolution of the Irish over the last 1000 years.

Coumeenoole, Dingle peninsula

Contents

The Legacy of Ancient Ireland

Mother Ireland

The land of Ireland – earth, rock and green mantle – has been a remarkable cradle to her people. That such a small island could produce so many exceptional scholars and writers seems unbelievable, especially when it is viewed as a geographical backwater on the furthest edge of Europe. One of the most important facets of the psyche of the Irish must be the love they bear for their damp little country. 'Mother Ireland' may be an anachronistic expression today – a left over from the inward looking Catholic attitudes of the de Valera era. Nevertheless, the concept expresses an age-old love for the land itself, which is invariably perceived as a feminine presence. Mountains such as the Paps – in mythology the breast of the Goddess Áine – in South Kerry and the Three Sisters of the Dingle Peninsula reflect the long lasting old perception of the land of Ireland as a woman.

Healy Pass, Beara Peninsula, West Cork

Since the arrival of the first farmers on the shores of Ireland nearly 7,000 years ago, the soil of Ireland has been sacred, a living organism which held the secrets of life and fertility. To the monk Blathmac – writing in the 8th century – the very trees of Ireland bled on the day that Christ was crucified.

"There was blood on the breasts of the world in the heights of every great forest."

This belief in the feminine power of the land has persisted throughout Irish history. The Celtic fertility goddesses of ancient Ireland survive today as the female saints of Pattern and Holy Well, whilst the four great annual pagan holidays have been Christianised into festivals like Halloween. Just as the basic settlement patterns of rural Ireland were established in prehistoric times, so were many of the underlying traditions and attitudes of the people. By the early Christian period – when monasteries and Viking ports were established as the first large urban settlements – Ireland had been an agricultural and pastoral society

for the best part of 6,000 years. This prehistoric legacy – the marriage of the Irish people to the earth – is still relevant, even in the age of television and the motor car.

The attachment of the Irish to their land is a continuing thread, which runs through Irish history and binds the past to the present. In 1948 an old Clare farmer – talking about local beliefs concerning fate and destiny – described an ancient tradition which encapsulated the symbolic relationship of man and the earth beneath his feet.

'I wish to mention the beliefs the old people had that it was laid out for a person, from the time the crown of his head came into the world, where his place of death was. For this person it was laid out that for him, or for her, the side of the road would be as a sod of death, for another the middle of the road, or out on the brown mountains, or in the loneliness of the wood or – as God save us from danger – a person could have as a sod of death a violent death.'

The legend of the three sods – of birth, death and burial – may well be traceable back to the religious ideas of the Stone Age farmers, who carefully covered their passage graves with alternating layers of stone and cut sods of earth. Yet nobody would suggest that the people of west Clare in 1948 were anything but strictly orthodox Catholics. However, their beliefs and ideas were the sum of changing influences over thousands of years, a complex mixture of new and old that set the boundaries of their character.

This may be compared to the landscape of Ireland, whose natural face has equally been changed by the arrival of each wave of settlers and colonists.

Neolithic Period

Ireland may seem insignificant when seen on a world map, but within her confines there is a surprising variety of landscape. The natural beauty of the island has been much modified by the interaction of man with the environment; many features that seem the result of natural growth or climactic change are also, at least in part, the result of human activity. During the 10,000 years or since the first hunter-gatherers crossed over to Ireland from Scotland, the appearance and dominant flora of the landscape have changed repeatedly. This process is ongoing. The wild fuchsia and rhododendron which grow so profusely in Irish hedgerows and through deciduous forests like those around Killarney, were introduced only 150 years or so ago, whilst such exotic domestic animals as llamas, sika deer and ostriches have made their appearance within recent decades. A rich growth of planted woodland now covers valleys like Glendalough (Wicklow), which in 19th century paintings are bare of trees. Vast plantations of pine trees have utterly changed the appearance of uplands that in living memory were bogs or heathery wastes.

St. Kevin's Church and Round Tower, Glendalough, Co. Wicklow

The introduction of farming into Ireland around 6,500 years ago stands as perhaps the single greatest leap forward in her history. The first agriculturists arrived on the north coasts and gradually moved south and westwards, until large areas of the country were under cultivation or tillage. Generally they avoided the marshy lowlands and kept to the wooded hills, hacking out clearings for their herds and crops by the

slash and burn method, then moving on when the soil was exhausted. Within a few centuries, communities of farmers began to establish themselves in northern and western areas, building themselves houses and erecting stone enclosures for their herds. Today many of these field systems have been covered by peat bog, as at the Ceide fields in County Mayo, where archaeologists have uncovered 4,500 year old stone walls.

It seems that by the end of the Neolithic period, around 4,000 years ago, the basic pattern of Irish farming until modern times had already been laid down. As it is today, the main emphasis was on beef and dairy farming – although the animals were oxen rather than cattle – with pigs, goats and sheep also common domestic animals. Cereal crops were not as important and much less ground was given over to their production. It is also likely that in some regions social organization had progressed beyond the family group to larger tribal units and rudimentary kingdoms ruled by priest-kings, even if it is unlikely that the scattered inhabitants of the island shared any sense of a common identity.

Court and Passage Graves

The most visible monuments of the Neolithic age in Ireland are the stone tombs built by these farmers. Examples of the most common early types, the 'court' grave and the 'passage' grave, may be seen in many counties in the northern half of Ireland. The distinct differences between these two forms of tomb suggest that they may reflect either separate waves of immigrants or differing social structures. Court graves are usually found in isolation, sometimes near to – or even built over – a prehistoric farmhouse. There is a fine court grace in the Ceide fields system, for example, which undoubtedly served the people who built the adjacent houses and stone wall systems. In court graves a circular or semi-circular area is recessed in front of a long walled chamber, which has been covered by a mound of earth or stone. Their elongated shape and structure has affinities with the long-barrows of England,

Carved stone at Newgrange, Co. Meath

11

indicating they are an Irish version developed by settlers who most probably arrived via southern Scotland. It seems likely that court graves were generally the communal burial place of a single family and its local descendants, a prehistoric version of the family plots that are still found in rural Irish graveyards.

Newgrange Megalithic Tomb, Co. Meath

Passage graves, on the other hand, pose a number of more complex questions. They belong to a category of prehistoric tomb found along the Atlantic coasts of Europe, where a passage leads into a chamber in which the bones or ashes of the dead are stored. The whole structure lies concealed beneath a circular mould held in place by curb stones. Although a number of passage graves stand alone, most are found in clusters, often on high places that are visible for miles around. This suggests that they formed ritual centres for quite large districts, a view supported by the impressive megalithic tombs at the World Heritage site of Brú na Bóinne in Co. Meath.

The passage graves at Knowth, Newgrange and Dowth rank amongst the finest prehistoric

Carved entrance stone at Newgrange, Co. Meath

monuments in the world. The huge restored mound of Newgrange, almost flying saucer-like on its ridge beside the river Boyne, is justly one of the great archaeological sites of Ireland. The triple spiral motif associated with Newgrange has come to symbolize the tomb as a huge achievement of Neolithic technology. Whilst single and double spirals are common motifs in Stone Age art, the triple spiral seems mainly to occur at this site, where it is carved on the entrance stone and inside the chamber of the passage grave. Although its exact meaning remains a mystery, some scholars believe the triple spiral symbolizes the cycle of birth, life and death.

It is tempting to see Newgrange and Knowth as 'royal' tombs, built for the rulers of primitive kingdom based on the Meath region. If this is so, then it marks an early step in the evolution of isolated farming communities into the 'kingdoms' into which Ireland was divided from the dawn of its recorded history up to the end of the 16th century.

Regardless of the truth of this theory, the long period between the building of the Boyne passage graves and the arrival of the Celts saw many cultural innovations, along with increased links with prehistoric societies in Britain and

Standing Stone, Dingle peninsula, Co. Kerry

the continent of Europe. Towards the end of the Neolithic age two new types of megalithic – or large stone – tomb became popular. The portal-tomb or dolmen, found mainly in the northwest of Ireland (although there are some fine examples in Leinster and around Galway Bay) seems to have been a simplified local variation of the court grave. The gallery grave, on the other hand, occurs mainly in the south and west of Ireland and may have been developed by new migrants arriving into Munster from western France.

The Bronze & Iron Age

The beginning of the Bronze Age, around 2000 BC, brought Ireland into a trading network that already existed throughout Europe. Substantial deposits of copper and gold made the island attractive to miners and metalworkers, encouraging a new wave of settlers. Stone circles, perhaps the most enchanting of all Irish prehistoric monuments, date largely from this period. Little is known about the purpose

Ogham Stone, Dunmore Head, Co. Kerry

of these mysterious sites, although archaeological evidence suggests they had some ritual significance and were often aligned to the sunrise and sunset. Considered with the large number of single standing stones and alignments that abound in many parts of Ireland, they suggest the expansion of a growing population into areas that were previously only thinly inhabited by semi-nomadic hunter gatherers.

From around 1200 BC onwards it appears that Ireland experienced a fresh wave of settlement, brought about by the expansion of peoples speaking an 'Indo-European' dialect, part of a linguistic family that is shared by almost all modern European languages, Iranian and Sanskrit amongst others. During the 'Dowris Period' around 700 BC much of the island seems to have been controlled by a rich aristocratic class, who made exquisite bronze weapons and possessed expansive imported luxuries like amber and jet necklaces.

By and large, however, Ireland was a simple pastoral society, where the number of cattle a man owned dictated his wealth and position in the community. The Celts of the La Téne culture, who are believed to have begun arriving around 500 BC, found themselves in a society that was not very dissimilar to those they knew in Britain and in Western Europe. Despite their divisions, it is not unreasonable to suspect that the people on the island by now shared some sense of Irishness, which transcended tribe or clan to include all those living within the confines of its shores. The Celts came in comparatively small numbers, as invaders or mercenaries; they relied on the quality of the iron weapons they carried to impose their authority on the natives of the island. Iron working certainly arrived in Ireland at the same time as the La Téne artefacts discovered by archaeologists, suggesting it was a Celtic introduction.

The spread of 'Celtic' culture and language probably occurred over a number of centuries and involved several waves of immigrants, some from Britain, some from France and Belgium and – according to legend at least – some from northern Spain. Earlier peoples already present were assimilated and lost their identities in new kingdoms and power groupings. Sites like Navan Fort and Tara – which were already important tribal centres – were taken over and became the capitals of quite large dynastic

Staigue Fort, Co. Kerry

kingdoms. On the treeless western seaboard, dry-walled promontory forts and circular cashels became common defences. Two types of lesser domestic dwellings came to the fore for smaller landowners. The crannóg - an artificial island built on a lake – had roots in the Bronze Age. It became more common in the Iron Age, surviving as a type until as late as 1600. The ring fort, a house within a palisaded circular bank of earth, seems to have evolved in the early centuries of the Christian era. Ring forts – which had the same function a modern farmhouse and its yard – remain the most common prehistoric monuments throughout the Irish countryside. Centuries after they were abandoned by their residents, the ring forts took on an important role in folklore as the haunt of the 'Little People' or Fairies. Even today they are respected in the Irish countryside and many farmers will not remove or interfere with them.

The long held belief in the Fairies has endured since pre-Christian times. Much of the folklore surrounding them may be traced back to the religious practices of the Celts. Prehistoric monuments and holy sites are often associated with fairy activity, for instance the great passage grave at Newgrange, which is said to be the home of the club-wielding Dagda, the High King of Fairyland. The most feared Fairy haunts in Ireland were probably Slievenamon ('The Mountain of the Women') and its subsidiary summit Sheegouna (the Fairy Mound of the Heifers) in Co. Tipperary.

Saint Patrick

Ireland was never incorporated into the Roman Empire but there is evidence that several Roman trading posts were established along the eastern coasts. The most enduring contribution made by Roman Britain to Ireland was the establishment of the Christian religion. Christianity was well established in England by A.D.400 and had almost certainly been brought to Ireland by individual migrant workers and soldiers returning home. It seems likely that by A.D.431 there were sizable Christian communities in some parts of Ireland, since in that year Germanus of Auxerre, who was trying to purge Pelagian heretics from the English Church, appointed one Palladius to be 'the first deacon of the Irish Christians'.

Ardmore, Co. Waterford

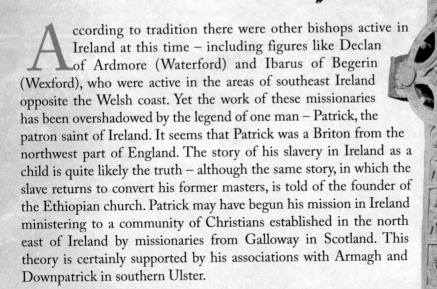

According to tradition there were other bishops active in Ireland at this time – including figures like Declan of Ardmore (Waterford) and Ibarus of Begerin (Wexford), who were active in the areas of southeast Ireland opposite the Welsh coast. Yet the work of these missionaries has been overshadowed by the legend of one man – Patrick, the patron saint of Ireland. It seems that Patrick was a Briton from the northwest part of England. The story of his slavery in Ireland as a child is quite likely the truth – although the same story, in which the slave returns to convert his former masters, is told of the founder of the Ethiopian church. Patrick may have begun his mission in Ireland ministering to a community of Christians established in the north east of Ireland by missionaries from Galloway in Scotland. This theory is certainly supported by his associations with Armagh and Downpatrick in southern Ulster.

However, his avowed purpose was the conversion of the pagan Irish. From his base in Armagh, the saint appears to have undertaken extensive missionary journeys, travelling Mayo, Donegal and other areas that were still entirely heathen. In his autobiographical 'Confessio' Patrick states that he had personally converted thousands of the Irish, a testament to both his persuasive powers and his stamina. The association of the saint's name with places such as Croagh Patrick and Lough Derg – which were probably sites of pagan worship – might be apocryphal. Nevertheless it suggests he had an important role in converting the north-western counties. A number of other famous legends, for instance those concerning his activities at Tara (Meath), are probably much later fabrications. Most likely the O'Neill rulers of Ulster, wishing to establish Patrick's church at Armagh as paramount in Ireland, invented them for propaganda purposes.

Saint Brigid

The conversion of Ireland was undoubtedly a longer and more complex process than the legend of Patrick allows. One of the notable features of Irish Christianity was the incorporation of Celtic gods and festivals into its fabric. The most famous example is St. Brigid of Kildare, cited as one of the founders of the Irish church in Leinster; Brigid was the most important Celtic fertility goddess, worshipped not only in Ireland but also across Europe in the pagan era. Her Christian saint's day – February 1- was shared with the pagan feast of Imbolc, the first of the four great annual holidays of Celtic Ireland. The perpetually lit sacred fire at the church of Brigid in Kildare was the continuation of a heathen practice that dated back to a time when the shrine was a pagan temple.

Beehive Huts , Skellig Michael

Monasteries

If the Christian beliefs of the people were tinged with a pagan element, the organization of the early Irish church developed along more orthodox lines. The monastic community rapidly became the heart of Irish Christianity, the central point from which radiated the renowned missionary impulse and scholarly wisdom of Ireland in the Dark Ages. The early monasteries were small and very austere, intended for those who wished to live removed from other men. They may be typified by remote little island settlements like Skellig Michael off the Kerry coast, which comprised only a simple church and a few beehive huts.

Clonmacnoise, Co. Offaly

Later on, however, monasteries were more ambitious and sometimes grew to become more like small towns, with abbots as powerful as kings ruling large populations of monks and lay servants. Many of the great monasteries of the Irish midlands, for example Clonmacnoise (Offaly), opened up huge new areas that had been thinly inhabited, clearing rough expanses of forest and marsh for cultivation and pasturage. The monasteries of early Ireland were not communal in organization like those of the Benedictines and mainland European orders. They consisted of a number of individuals who carried out their religious observances in private, assembling only for church services and to help administer the monastery.

Nevertheless, large foundations like Glendalough (Co. Wicklow) had a number of important social and religious functions. Despite its seeming remoteness, this monastery stands at the hub of a network of roads that cross the Wicklow Mountains from east to west and north to south. By the 10th century a large walled settlement had grown up around the lakes where St. Kevin had established himself as a hermit. Glendalough, with its round tower, churches and crosses, attracted many pilgrims and was also a market and trade centre for the region. Yet in addition to the main church and shrine of St. Kevin, smaller monastic enclosures in the valley were provided for monks who wished to live in isolation.

Irish monasteries of the early Christian era became famous for their scholarship. Their illuminated manuscripts, most famously the Book of Kells (now in the library of Trinity College, Dublin), are still objects of wonder, as are the exquisite chalices and examples of ecclesiastical metal displayed in our National Museum. With the flowering of the Irish Church and the journeys of missionary monks to Britain and the Continent of Europe, Ireland's long prehistory drew to a close as the island slowly emerged on the stage of recorded history.

Clonmacnoise, Co. Offaly

The West Of Ireland And The Atlantic Coast

Sea, Sky and Mountain

The Cliffs of Moher, Co. Clare

The winds that blow so frequently over Ireland have played a major part in shaping both her landscape and history. They are a constant factor in the climate and there are few days in the year when the air is still. Savage autumn gales from the Atlantic, icy gusts crossing Europe from Siberia and warm African breezes originating in the Sahara, all end up on the Irish shores. These never ending pattern of winds cause the changes in light which make the landscape hazy and muted on one day and bright and clear on another.

Doo Lough, Co. Mayo

Ireland, particularly in its western regions, is a land of horizons made glorious by towering, cloudy skies. The artist Paul Henry captured this aspect brilliantly in his landscape paintings, placing huddled cottages against dark hills and mountains dwarfed by huge skies. More than anything else, perhaps, the relationship between the western coasts and the world beyond is defined by the vast emptiness that stretches to the western horizon from cliffs where the land abruptly meets the wild Atlantic seas.

The unique western Irish landscape must be amongst the most beautiful in the world. Since man first arrived on these coasts, great forests of oak and elm have disappeared from the slopes of the mountains, whilst blanket bogs have formed a shroud over arable lands that once held the settlements of Neolithic pastoralists. Yet the bones of the land remain the same; now, as then, the impressive peaks still rise from the western edge of Ireland to break the flatness of her central plain.

The Gallarus Oratory, Dingle, Co. Kerry

Like human beings everywhere, the Irish have given a central role to mountains in their mythology as the homes of the Gods. Yet the nearness of the comparatively low Irish peaks suggests an uncommon intimacy between the deities of the high places and

21

their worshippers below. Mount Brandon, the second highest mountain in Ireland, barely exceeds 3000 feet in height and can be climbed in a few hours from the Dingle peninsula beneath. On its windy mist covered summit is one of the great holy places in Ireland, dedicated to the shadowy figure of Brendan the Navigator, a 7th century abbot whose legend blends memories of real voyages by early Christian monks with Celtic myths about the western Isles of the Dead.

The annual pilgrimage to the oratory and crumbling well on top of Mount Brandon is undoubtedly extremely ancient in origin, quite likely as old as the habitation of man on the Dingle peninsula itself. But the appeal of the peak is far greater than its historical associations. On the rare occasions that the mists clear the summit, it offers a bird's eye view of the west of Ireland, laying out the loneliness of the mountainous coastline against the vast and frightening expanses of the Atlantic Ocean. This view encapsulates a basic truth about Ireland, that for millennia it stood on the rim of the known world, between Europe on one hand and the ocean – which divides all men from the unattainable realms of the spirit – on the other.

The western isolation of the Atlantic coasts of Ireland has made them the last cultural outpost of the European continent. Until modern times, the traditional life style of its fishermen and pastoralists remained essentially prehistoric, with archaic practices such as rundale farming (the communal sharing of fields) and transhumance (moving animals to upland summer pastures) still common. The traditional western cottage – the long-house – is derived from primitive thatch and stone dwellings that have changed little from Stone Age types, whilst corbelled stone huts were still being built for outhouses until recent decades. Human beings have lived on these coasts for a very long time, moving into the region from the east, south and north.

The Pier at Dunquin, Dingle, Co. Kerry

The towns and villages of the West are for the most part comparatively small, and rarely more than a few hundred years old. The exceptions are ports like Limerick, Galway and Sligo and towns such as Askeaton (Limerick) and Athenry (Galway), established by Anglo-Norman colonists along the Shannon estuary or the western margins of the central plains. In the Middle Ages these cities and walled burghs were on the western frontier of Feudal Europe, isolated islands of urban civilization in a hinterland dominated by 'wild' Irish and 'degenerate' Norman chieftains. The ravages of war and time have ensured that little but ruins remain from this medieval heritage; today Georgian and Victorian buildings dominate the streets of town and city alike in the West of Ireland.

A Birds Eye View of Ireland

Despite the charming ambience of the quaint West Cork villages or the small market towns of North Donegal, the settlements of the Atlantic seaboard are dwarfed by the wild landscape in which they are set. Even the spires and slate

Rock formation, Beara, Co. Cork

roofs of sizable towns like Dingle (Kerry) or Clifden (Galway) seem toy-like afterthoughts when set beneath towering mountains and wild skies. Perhaps no earthbound human eye can catch the essential unity of the Atlantic coasts. From south to north, stony wastes or patchy areas of human cultivation separate range upon range of stark mountains. Perhaps only from the skies above would it be possible to comprehend the awesome harmony of these wild shores, bounded between rocky hills and bogland on one side, and the endless reaches of the ocean on the other.

View of the Blasket Islands, Co. Kerry

To a migratory bird, blown by fierce winds over the empty Atlantic from Africa or the Americas, the south western margins of Ireland might first appear as a distant speck on the horizon – a shadowy hint that the ocean was about to meet land again. Eventually this hazy smudge on the infinite grey of the sea materializes into a rock coast where the sea carves deep inlets between mountainous peninsulas. Scattered islands, sprinkled a few miles offshore, mark the tentative western limits of Ireland. From the air they seem insignificant, these tiny specks of rock and soil against the bulk of the mainland, yet in a very real sense they stand as a westernmost

Atlantic Puffins

boundary of human habitation in Europe. Some – like Skellig Michael off the coast of Kerry – seem almost uninhabitable, yet are spotted with the ruined churches and beehive huts of reclusive Irish monks who lived there a thousand years ago. On others, such as the Blaskets off the Dingle peninsula, the slowly disintegrating cottages of populations who left almost within living memory bear mute witness to the difficulties of sustaining life in so isolated and impoverished an environment.

Yet a number of these small islands are still inhabited; they form some of the remotest communities in Western Europe, often completely cut off for days at a time in stormy weather. The Aran Islands, off Galway Bay further north, typify the cultural depth of these ancient societies and their archaic traditions and life styles. Clusters of long-house cottages and tiny stone field hark back to a type of farming that in prehistoric times was the norm throughout much of Europe. Gaelic, the language of the people who dwell on the islands, is the oldest north of the Alps. Despite their remoteness, the Aran Islands have had a profound influence on the mainstream of Irish cultural life, especially during the vital era in the early 1900's, when they provided inspiration to the dramatist John Synge and such artists as Jack Yeats and Paul Henry.

West Cork and Kerry

The western islands lie off coasts that are beautiful but forbidding; presenting harsh expanses of bare rock and rough grass, with few trees larger than gnarled, wind twisted thorns or hazel scrub. Ireland – as every Irish school child knows – is shaped like a sitting bear, with its back to Britain and

Sea Cliffs, Aran Islands

its upper and lower legs facing west. The lower legs, comprising the mountainous sandstone promontories of West Cork and Kerry, are deeply indented by the sea and bordered for the most part by cliffs and stony islets. These barren coasts have little to offer man, but in summer serve as the breeding ground for thousands of seabirds. Cormorants, Shags, Razorbills, Guillemots and Kittiwake cram onto the ledges, whilst Puffins and Gannets nest on the rocky islands and headlands. Gull colonies add to the general noise and air of excitement, leaving ocean-wandering Manx Shearwaters and Storm Petrels to seek the peace of the remotest islands and rocks for their annual breeding visit ashore. The annual departure of these feathered visitors heralds the coming of winter, when the nearly deserted cliffs are buffeted by ferocious gales and rainstorms.

Lakes of Killarney, Co. Kerry

Inland from the cliffs a wall of mountains rises, broken by valleys and coastal strips where fields, farmhouses and the occasional small town or hamlet mark the presence of man on the landscape. In the extreme southwest the hilly and verdant Cork countryside peters out in the narrow Mizen and Durrus peninsulas, with their distinctive two-dormer, 'one and a half story' farmhouses. Further north, beyond Bantry with its imposing mansion on the hill above the town, the country becomes more rugged. The lush vegetation of Glengarriff – with the gardens of Garinish Island like an emerald in the bay – is a green splash against the desolate mountains of the Beara peninsula. The thin line of the road connecting the southern and northern shores of the peninsula is clearly visible. It winds in great serpentine loops over the summit of the Healy Pass, then descends to Kenmare Bay and the towering mountains of the Iveragh peninsula.

Although the mountains of west Kerry are not high by European standards, they soar upward in serried ranges to culminate in the magnificent peaks of the MacGillicuddy's Reeks, Ireland's highest mountains. Beneath them, the Iveragh peninsula is mostly a stark expanse of bare rock, raised bog and heather. Only where the mountains break can strips of forest and green fields be glimpsed. Whilst there are quite lush belts of vegetation around Kenmare Bay and along the coast further north, the westernmost edge of the peninsula is stark and poor. Inland, the enchanted lakes of Killarney are set in a valley between the Reeks and the hilly

Garinish Island, Glengarriff, West Cork

area known as the Glens, which separates Kerry from the rest of Munster. Ross Castle and Muckross House – the imposing monuments of the medieval Gaelic lords of the region and their Anglo-Irish successors – stand out impressively on the lakeside, whilst patches of oak forest interspersed with wild rhododendrons cling to the valleys and lower slopes of the peaks.

Ross Castle, Killarney, Co. Kerry

North of Killarney, the Dingle Peninsula is yet more barren, dominated by the humped crest of Mount Brandon and the spine of hills that runs down its entire length. The white beach and sand dunes of Inch Strand stretch out into the sea south of the mountains, but further along the coast the impressive storm tossed rocks and cliffs of Slea Head provide some of the finest scenery in Ireland. Out to sea lie the fabled Blasket Islands, deserted since 1955 but before that one of the last great repositories of Gaelic culture. At the tip of the peninsula the mountains break, leaving a narrow toenail of comparatively flat arable land between Dingle town and the bulk of Brandon itself. This cramped area is another nexus of tradition, still largely Gaelic speaking but struggling to retain its identity against the tides of tourism. Thirty years ago Dingle was a small fishing port and market centre, where it was not uncommon to find flocks of sheep tethered to lampposts on Fair Day and Irish was the everyday language. Today you are more likely to hear English, German or French in its cosmopolitan restaurants and craft shops.

Coumeenoole Beach, Dingle, Co. Kerry

The Shannon Estuary & Clare

By now a north-flying bird would have traversed the rugged sandstone peninsulas of West Cork and Kerry. Beyond the sprawling conglomerate of Tralee, the flatter lands of north Kerry give a more placid landscape of low hills and farming country which stretches to the Shannon estuary. At this point the inhospitable Atlantic coasts break, offering a route along the great river into the green heart of Ireland. The southern shore of the estuary is hilly in places, but largely good agricultural land, its large fields golden with hay or filled with well fed cattle. The signs of human habitation are much stronger, with more houses and fair-sized market towns, often clustered around some ruined castle or friary. South and east the countryside rolls into the rich farmlands of Cork and Tipperary, whilst along the shores of the estuary the mudflats provide a rich autumn feeding ground for migratory ducks and geese.

Muckross House, Killarney, Co. Kerry

The flight of our imaginary bird now takes him over the first city he has passed on the journey, the Viking foundation of Limerick, built where the river approaches the sea. The Shannon, with its lakes and reedy expanses, is both a road inland and a wall between the east and west sides of the island. For much of its 240 mile length the countryside around turns its back on the river. The few substantial towns on its banks are found at the points where it is crossed by bridges or joined by canals from the north and east. As a highway for commerce the river is situated on the wrong side of Ireland. Limerick, still largely a Georgian city, has declined from its heyday during the age of canals in the 18th and 19th centuries. Nevertheless, Shannon Airport is a few miles north and contributes to the city's economy.

Bunratty Castle, Co. Clare

On the far side of Limerick, Bunratty Castle and the thatched cottages of its Folk Village stand guard over the approaches to the river and city. Further north, beyond the towering turrets of Dromoland Castle and the substantial Anglo-Norman

Thatched cottage, Bunratty, Co. Clare

town of Ennis, the soft green fringes of Clare soon give way to the harsher terrain of the Burren. The bare limestone summits rise to about a thousand feet, a grey stone desert bereft of vegetation except for the unique array of flora in the soil deposits in their cracks and sheltered places. No rivers run down from the hills, for the rain that falls on them is carried through fissures to a system of underground streams, which emerge lower down to fertilize patches of grassland and deciduous forest. These subterranean waters have carved cave systems beneath the surface, such as the beautiful Ailwee Caves, situated on the northern edge of the Burren above Ballyvaughan.

At the edges of the limestone plateau, where it meets the sea, flat beds of shale and sandstone have followed above the limestone to form one of the great natural spectacles of Ireland. For eight miles the Cliffs of Moher sweep and curve along the coast without interruption. A small 19th century tower marks their highest point of nearly 670 feet from bottom to top. Away to the west of the Cliffs, the Aran Islands stretch out seawards, whilst to the north the limestone wastes of Black Head lead into the wide expanses of Galway Bay.

Galway & the West

In an eastward direction the stony hills of north Clare slowly merge into Ireland's central plains. In the distance, across the bay, the city of Galway straddles the river Corrib as it rushes into the sea. It is too far away to make out the details of this exquisite city, but the bungalows and modern houses snaking on the roads that lead into the surrounding countryside mark its growth in recent years. The street plan and tall old houses in the centre are a legacy of the walled and towered medieval city, but new buildings and developments indicate that modern Galway has become a metropolis, even if a fairly modest one by European standards.

The Burren, Co. Clare

Sunset, the magnificent Cliffs of Moher, Co. Clare

The Corrib River rushes down to the sea from the wide waters of Lough Corrib, which with Lough Mask further north, forms a natural frontier between west Galway and the rest of Ireland. The fabled Connemara terrain – so beloved by artists and writers – is a mixture of flat bogs and patches of more fertile land bounded by a deeply indented coastline. To the west it is Gaelic speaking and retains traces of old clachan settlements, whilst stone wall systems and a sprinkling of cottages proclaim the modern presence of man. The few larger settlements of west Galway – like the freshwater fishing town of Oughterard or the coastal village of Spiddal – show themselves here and there as humble cluster of roofs and spires in the vast broken landscape. Further north again the scenery becomes even more impressive as the pyramidical peaks of the Twelve Bens mountains becomes begin to dominate he horizon. In fertile low-lying area near their southern edge, the busy tourist town of Clifden shelters besides its muddy creek, its church spires dwarfed by the surrounding peaks.

Beyond Clifden the scenery becomes wildly spectacular as the bird passes over tiny Letterfrack and enters the Connemara National Park. Small patches of forest and farmland interrupt huge expanses of bogland from which majestic peaks rise to 2000 feet. The sea has

Clifden, Connemara

carved deep bays and into the coast and narrow glacial lakes nestle into the valley beneath the mountains. At the foot of a cliff besides one of these loughs, a majestic white building stands proudly above a fringe of deciduous trees – the dream castle of Kylemore Abbey, built by a Manchester speculator for his wife. Peak after peak rears its stately head on every side. At last, a few miles beyond the deep inlet of Killary fjord, the mountains fall away into lower hills – leaving the single stark peak of Croagh Patrick to dominate the approaches to Clew Bay and Westport.

The mountain is the holiest in Ireland, and the Pilgrims Road to its summit appears as a deep scar slashed upon its raw flanks. Towards the north it looks down upon Clew Bay and its myriad of tiny islands and the dark bulk of Mayo beyond – looming mountain ranges and rock coasts hammered by the wild Atlantic gales. The pretty little 18th century town of Westport – designed by the great Georgian architect Wyatt – is an island of civilization amidst this wild grandeur, a gateway between the agricultural hinterland of Connaught and the inhabited strips of land stretching along the margins of the bay itself. In the 16th century this was pirate country, famous as the lair of the remarkable Gráinne O'Maille, who ruled the seas around Connaught from her castle on the Rockfleet Bay.

Several inhabited islands lie off these coasts. Clare Island, the mouth of Clew Bay, is associated with Gráinne O'Maille, whom some believe is buried in its small abbey. The island is marked by the ruins of a tower house and a lighthouse that was closed down in 1965. Achill Island, further north just off the

Croagh Patrick Mountain, Co. Mayo

Mayo coast, is barely an island at all; since 1887 it has been connected to the mainland by a short bridge. Here are the mighty cliffs of Croaghaun, at 688 metres (2257 feet) the third highest sea-cliffs in Europe. Several groups of house ruins are visible, the remains of clachan settlements abandoned after the Famine, or following mass evictions by greedy landlords. Such groups of broken stone walls and tottering gables are found at many points along the Atlantic shores of Ireland. A few mark the remains of mining or quarrying villages but most are the visible aftermath of the catastrophic potato blight of the 1840s.

Glencolumbkille, Co. Donegal

Beyond the beautiful Mullet Peninsula, Benwee Head and the cliff bound shores of north Mayo, the traces of ancient human habitation make their mark on the landscape. At the Ceide Fields on the northern coast of the County, an area of stripped away bog reveals the field walls, tombs and houses of farmers who settled the area 4500 years ago. As the bird continues along the coast into Sligo it reaches one of the cradles of prehistoric man in Ireland, the beacon-like hill of Knockarea. The great cairn on its summit – in legend the burial place of the ancient Queen Maebh – is almost certainly a passage grave, whilst the remains of the largest prehistoric cemetery in Europe are nestled around Carrowmore at its feet.

Sligo & Donegal

The bird, still flying north, passes over Sligo, the third largest city along the western seaboard of Ireland after Limerick and Galway. To the northeast, beneath the imposing bulk of Kings Mountain,

Traditional cottage, Glencolumbkille, Co. Donegal

a small sliver of blue marks Glencar Lake, home of W. B. Yeat's 'Lake Isle of Inisfree'. Next in view appears the spectacular table-top mountain of Ben Bulben. From its flat summit, the vast granite expanses of Donegal – quartzite peaks rising range upon range to the tip of the island – afford a view rivalling any seen on the odyssey to this point. Beyond the small town of Donegal, with its restored castle and shattered Franciscan friary, two main routes lead into the hinterland. The first road goes northeast, joining Donegal to Letterkenny at the base of Lough Swilly – leaving the bulk of the county to the west and north. The second route leads west, following the coast past the fishing village of Killybegs. Far beyond its trawlers and the armies of gulls wheeling over its processing plants, the road peters out at the remote valley of Glencolmkille, near the westernmost point of the county.

Glencolmkille is the last stop on a road that leads only to the vast and intimidating Donegal coast, onto which so many ships of the Spanish Armada were blown and destroyed in 1588. Twisting hill roads connect the little towns on the shore to each other and the interior, often crossing huge areas of uninhabited bog and bleak mountain passes. Ardara, Dungloe and the other settlements are separated by breathtaking scenery, the peaks rising until they culminate in the huge bulk of Errigal, nearly 2500 feet high. In the 19th century the life of this countryside was unbelievably primitive, even by Irish standards. Today it is still a land of white cottages and hill farms, its few wooded and arable areas almost like oases in the folds of the boggy mountains.

At Malin Head, on the remote Inishowen peninsula, the northernmost point of the Irish mainland is reached. On either side two great inlets of the sea – Lough Swilly and Lough Foyle – provide shelter from the Atlantic storms. At the base of the peninsula – just across the border in Northern Ireland – the little city of Derry/Londonderry nestles within the circuit of its walls. Although the town dates from the plantation of Ulster in the 1600's, the haven on which it stands has been a northern gateway into the almost impenetrable interior since ancient times.

Derry-Londonderry

The Causeway Coast & the Glens of Antrim

The bird has left the traditional boundary of the West of Ireland long behind by the time it crosses Malin Head. Even so, the stretch of coast that continues along the northern edge of the island of Ireland is a natural extension of the Donegal coast. Geologically, this part of Ulster is dominated by great flows of basalt, overlaying deposits of chalk, clays and redstone.

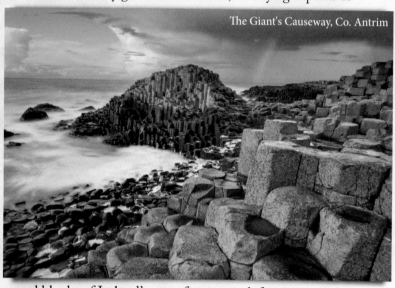

The Giant's Causeway, Co. Antrim

As a result the appearance of the coast changes after Inishowen. Turning east, the bird finds itself heading along a craggy dark coast past the remarkable rock castle of Dunluce, once the chief fortress of the Scottish MacDonnells who ruled this coast. Following a line of sandy beaches it eventually reaches the spectacular basalt cliffs of the so called Causeway Coast. Very soon the octagonal blocks of Ireland's most famous rock formation – the Giant's Causeway – are passed. Out to sea the little island of Rathlin rides the waves like a ship. Around Fair Head warm red sandstone predominate in the sea cliffs, topped by flat moorland which preserves Neolithic settlements beneath its peat. The deserted area is an important haunt of gulls and other birds, notably raptors like the buzzard and the rare golden eagle.

The long flight around the Atlantic coast is nearly over. The last stop of our imaginary bird is the Glens of Antrim – nine deep glacial valleys facing the Mull of Kintyre in Scotland. Here it might be said that the Atlantic ends and the Irish Sea begins. Before the 1830's – when the road that now sweeps around the coast was built – the Glens were isolated from the rest of Ireland by the difficult terrain of the Antrim plateau. They were in closer contact with the areas across the North Channel in Scotland than the rest of Ulster, keeping the Gaelic language and old way of life well into the 19th century.

The waters off these shores are known as the sea of Moy. There could be no more suitable ending to a bird's journey than to recall it was on these waters that the Children of Lir spent three hundred years of their exile as swans.

Dunluce Castle, Co. Antrim

Dublin & the East Coast

Ireland's Gateway

The east and south coasts of Ireland present a very different face to the world than the west. For much of their length these shores are open to the interior and a series of deep bays and river estuaries offer fine harbours for shipping. This is particularly true of the shoreline facing North Wales and the north-western region of England. From the Mourne Mountains in southern Ulster to the Wicklow Mountains south of Dublin, the flat central plain reaches out to meet the sea. Two river systems – the Boyne and the Liffey – offer access to some of the best arable land in Ireland. This region has long been the most accessible gateway into the island from England and Wales. Its most important city, Dublin, has been the capital of the country and its major cultural and economic centre since the early Middle Ages.

The river Liffey at dusk, Dublin City

The Viking Era

The history of Dublin reflects the changes brought about in Ireland by the domination of England over the last 1000 years. Its beginnings date back to the Viking era, when Ireland's turbulent self-contained society of little kingdoms and powerful monasteries was turned upside down by Norse invaders. They came first as pirates around A.D. 800, swooping down on coastal monasteries and sailing up the Boyne and other rivers to loot inland. Towards the middle of the century they turned from robbery to conquest, making determined efforts to establish themselves on Irish soil. Initially the Vikings failed in this attempt, but after A.D. 900 a second wave of invasion succeeded in establishing a number of permanent enclaves along the eastern and southern coasts and at Limerick on the mouth of the Shannon.

These scattered Viking settlements became the first real towns in Ireland. Even today the names of many Irish ports hint at their Scandinavian origins. Waterford, for example, was originally 'Wether Fjord' – the inlet of the sheep, referring to its major export. Wexford was 'esker fjord', the inlet by the sandbar and Arklow 'Arnkel's Meadow' after some long forgotten Norse farmer. Most of these Norse towns – except the important trading city of Limerick in the west – were situated on the natural harbours of the Irish and Celtic seas, facing towards Viking colonies in the Isle of Man, Northern England and the Scottish Isles. They were part of a network which reached out from Scandinavia westwards to Iceland, Greenland and beyond, and to the east stretched across the Baltic and led through the rivers of Russia to the Black Sea, Constantinople and the Middle East.

Dublin – 'the Black Pool'- was an important international emporium centre on these routes. Viking ships are believed to have used the site as a temporary camp as early as 841, and by the 900's a thriving town had grown up on the slopes between the river Liffey and the present day Christ Church Cathedral. The discovery of fragments of Byzantine gold cloth and Arabic coins in Dublin suggest how far flung its connections were during the period. Local industries included exquisite silver working; examples of the heavy 'thistle broochs' made by Dublin craftsmen have been unearthed in Norway and other Viking areas. The hinterland of the city appears to have been heavily settled by Norse colonists, the area north of Dublin becoming known as Fingal in Irish, or 'land of the golden haired foreigners'. In the 10th century the Kingdom of Dublin became one of the most powerful Viking states in the British Isles. Excavations at Wood Quay in Dublin showed the Norse city to have been of wooden construction, with its small houses contained in fenced yards and open workshops lining its wooden paved streets. The city was fortified, originally with earthen ramparts, then later by a stone wall. By A.D. 1000 its inhabitants were largely Christian and in 1034 King Sitric founded the cathedral of Christ Church.

Christ Church Cathedral, Dublin City

Outside of the Norse Cities the Irish Kingdoms changed little. Kings ruled from rock strongholds like Dunamase (Laois) and Cashel (Tipperary), whilst the large monasteries at Lismore, Clonmacnoise, Kells and elsewhere retained their great power. Yet, inevitably, the establishments of wider contacts with the world outside opened Ireland to new influences from England and the mainland of Europe. The first

The Rock of Cashel, Co. Tipperary

major developments took place in the Celtic Church, which had been corrupted by too close political ties with secular rulers. Under the aegis of Malachy – the reforming archbishop of Armagh – the Cistercian order of monks set up an abbey at Mellifont (Louth) in 1142. The order, which followed an austere discipline based on that of the Benedictines, became very successful in Ireland. No less than thirty-nine Cistercian monasteries were founded in Ireland, either from the parent house at Mellifont or from English abbeys. These included such important abbeys as Jerpoint (Kilkenny), Boyle (Sligo), Holy Cross (Tipperary) and Tintern Manor (Wexford). Most of these foundations were placed in remote areas away from other settlements and were self-sufficient, living off food they grew and reared on their own lands.

Jerpoint Abbey, Co. Kilkenny

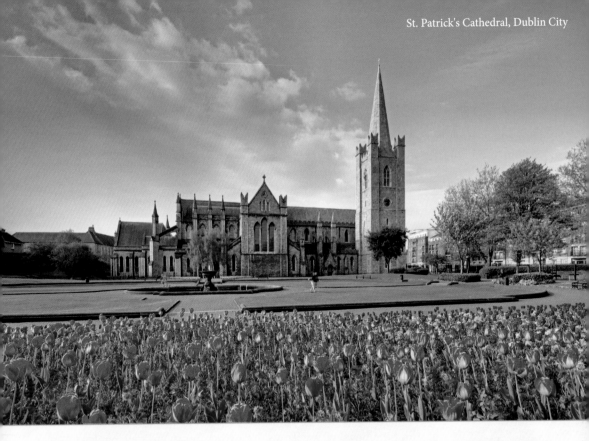

A few years before the arrival of the Cistercians, King Cormac MacCarthy decided to have a church built on the Rock of Cashel, which had been given to the Church in 1101. Rather than use Irish builders, he imported English masons to erect a church in the Romanesque style. Cormac's Chapel still stands and is today considered the finest 12th century building in Ireland. Influenced by its example, an Irish version of Romanesque architecture flourished and replaced earlier styles.

Medieval Ireland

The Cistercians and other orders like the Augustinians were the precursors of a new wave of invaders who would eventually destroy the old Celtic order. In 1169 Dermot MacMurrough, the exiled king of Leinster invited Norman mercenaries from west Wales and the Bristol area to help him recover his kingdom. The first advance party landed in Bannow Bay (Wexford) in 1169, to be followed by larger forces under the command of 'Strongbow' – the Earl of Pembroke. The Normans rapidly captured the Viking towns of Wexford and Wicklow and moved on to take Dublin, which

Strongbow's Tomb, Christ Church Cathedral, Dublin City

43

became the centre of their activities. In 1171, Henry II, King of England brought a large army to Ireland and established his sovereignty over the island, establishing an English domination that would not be broken for over 700 years. Following his departure, Norman barons began to seize more land from the Irish chieftains, rapidly overrunning large tracts of the countryside. Dublin became the centre of the Norman colony and its large and gloomy castle the administrative headquarters of the English Justiciar, or viceroy.

The Normans rebuilt Christ Church Cathedral after they captured the city in 1169 and in 1190 a second cathedral – St.Patrick's – was founded just outside the town wall. The bustling medieval city, with its craft workshops and merchants houses, spread out southwards from the River Liffey. With the exception of parts of St. Audoen's church (Cornmarket) and a nearby arch and piece of the city wall, most of Medieval Dublin has been replaced by later buildings and even the castle and its Cathedrals have been much rebuilt.

Rothe House, Kilkenny City

Cahir Castle, Co. Tipperary

By 1300 the Norman colony dominated most of Ireland outside of the far west and the interior of Ulster. Already the French and English landowners on its frontiers were intermarrying with native ruling families, and beginning to adopt Irish dress and customs. In 1315 a Scottish army under the command of Edward Bruce invaded Ireland and caused great ruination over the countryside. The destruction of towns, villages and castles badly weakened the settled areas under English rule. The Irish experienced a military resurgence and began reclaiming lands they had previously lost. The process of decay was accelerated by the effects of the Black Death around 1350, and by the end of the century much of Ireland had passed out of the control of the King's Justiciar in Dublin. With the exception of a small area around Dublin, the so-called 'Pale' from the wooden wall that marked its boundary, power now mainly lay in the hands of Irish chiefs and renegade Anglo-Norman lineages like the Burkes and Fitzgeralds.

There was a revival in building during the 15th century, and many friaries and tower houses were erected throughout the Irish countryside. Merchants in the walled towns lived in fine homes like the Rothe House in Kilkenny, perhaps the finest example of late medieval domestic architecture in Ireland, whilst the Lords and Chieftains of ruling families built strong castles at Bunratty, Blarney, Cahir and elsewhere. The Irish language had replaced English almost everywhere on the island.

Blarney Castle, Co. Cork

The 16th & 17th Centuries

The two hundred years between 1500 and 1700 saw the end of the old Irish and Norman ruling families and their replacement by a new aristocracy of English and Scottish landlords. By 1605 the powerful Earl of Desmond in Munster and the independent O'Neill and O'Donnell Lords of Ulster had been conquered, along with many lesser chieftains. Under the Tudor and Stuart dynasties attempts were made to pacify Ireland by planting English and Scottish settlers on lands confiscated from Irish rebels. In Leinster and Munster, new English landowners took over existing castles such as Lismore (Waterford) or built themselves fortified houses like Mallow (Cork) and Huntingdon (Carlow). Some Irish lords who had surrendered to the new order also

built new homes, for instance Richard Burke, Earl of Clanricarde. His magnificent house at Portumna (Galway), built in 1618, heralded a new era in Irish domestic architecture.

In Hoe Signo Vinces

Lamh Derg Eirin

By far the most important plantations took place in Ulster. Before the defeat in 1603 of the great rebellion led by Hugh O'Neill, the heartlands of Ulster had been the most Gaelic part of Ireland. Behind the barrier of mountains, drumlins and lakes which divided Ulster from the rest of Ireland, the life of the common people had changed little in 1000 years. However, the 'Flight of the Earls' in 1607 – which saw the leading lords of Ulster flee to Spain – led to over a half million acres of profitable land being made available for settlement.

The Ulster plantations changed the face of Ireland permanently, as large areas of the province were settled by Protestants from England and the lowlands of Scotland. The Colonists survived several rebellions by the native Irish in the 17th century, and eventually grew to outnumber their Catholic neighbours in the northern part of the island. Before the Plantation there were few towns or even stone buildings in Ulster. In 1624 Derry/Londonderry, the last walled city built in Europe, became one of the first and most important foundations of the Plantation. On Lough Erne in Fermanagh the Maguire castle at Enniskillen was rebuilt and became the centre of another important town. Throughout the countryside there was a flurry of building activity as fortified houses and villages were erected on confiscated lands. Some of the planters appear to have brought their own masons, since 17th century castles like Monea (Fermanagh), Tully (Fermanagh) and Ballygally (Tyrone) have very strong Scottish features.

ublin and the rest of Ireland experienced equally great changes after 1600. The 17th century saw the continuation of a cycle of wars and confiscations that had been started by Henry VIII in 1534, when his forces crushed the Earldom of Kildare. By the early 1700s only one seventh of the land of Ireland remained in Catholic hands. The rest had passed to a new Protestant landowning class, introduced from England and Scotland. Roman Catholics – who made up the bulk of the population – were excluded from political and economic life by a series of 'Penal Laws'. Power rested firmly in the hands of the 'Ascendancy', the descendents of Protestant English colonists who settled in Ireland during the era of the Tudors, Stuarts and William of Orange. The Irish Parliament, which was based in Dublin, became the principle organ through which the views of this elite minority were passed onto the English government in London.

Thatched cottages, Adare Village, Co. Limerick

Georgian & Victorian Ireland

The years of peace after 1700 led to great developments in Ireland, although economic progress was blocked by English controls on exports. Landlords grew rich from the rents of their tenants or began improving their lands. Many of the better Anglo-Irish landlords developed model villages near to or on their estates, providing better constructed homes than primitive mud cabins, along with schools and other amenities for their tenants. Sizable towns like Mitchelstown (Cork) and Birr (Offaly) owe their foundation to local landlords, as do the picturesque villages of Enniskerry (Wicklow), Adare (Limerick) and Tyrells Pass (Westmeath). The rebuilding of existing medieval centres gathered momentum at the same time. The towers and clay and wattle houses which were the typical domestic dwellings of Cork, Galway and other cities, were replaced by Georgian and 19th century town houses. Today, even moderate sized towns like Mullingar (Westmeath), Cashel (Tipperary) and Cahir (Tipperary) have some notably fine Georgian public and domestic architecture on their streets.

Thatched cottage, Bunratty, Co. Clare

The rural landscape of eastern and southern Ireland began to take on its present appearance in the Georgian era. The hedgerows and lines of trees that typify the field systems of the more fertile farming regions of Leinster and Munster, were laid down at this time. Better off tenant farmers began replacing their turf or clay cabins with stone farmhouses and cottages. The mass of the rural poor, depending for their food on potatoes grown on tiny plots of land, were not rehoused till much later. By the 1840s agricultural land was dangerously overcrowded, resulting in the terrible

Ruin of Famine Village, Achill Island, Co. Mayo

devastation of the Great Famine after potato crops were destroyed by blight; death and emigration reduced the population by more than half. In the late Victorian era, after 1890, a determined effort by benevolent landlords, the Congested Districts Board and Local and County Councils provided thousands of subsidized cottages for farm labourers and tenants, many of whom who were still living in impermanent hovels.

The building of canal systems linking Dublin to the Shannon and other river systems encouraged economic development. The Grand Canal – opened in 1804 – began at the Ringsend Basin

Grand Canal, Co. Kildare

in Dublin and crossed the middle of Ireland to meet the Shannon at the once busy river port of Shannon Harbour. The Royal Canal took a more northerly route from Dublin, going via Mullingar to join the river at Richmond Harbour north of Loch Ree. In the north, other canals joined the Shannon to the Erne Navigation. The upgrading

and improvement of roads matched the development of canals. Stagecoach routes were established, making it possible for travellers to move between towns with ease. Coaching Inns like the famous Brazen Head in Dublin provided them with accommodation and food on the way. New stone bridges were built and earlier medieval bridges like that erected by the Cistercians at Abbeyleix (Laois) restored or replaced. There was also an increase in industrial activity throughout the countryside, with the erection of Linen, Woollen or Grain mills at many locations. Lighthouses were built around dangerous coasts, and harbours and quays built or improved. In the 1800's magnificent new piers were erected at Kingstown (Dun Laoghaire), built with granite from the quarry at Dalkey Hill, two miles away.

On October 9, 1834 the first railway in Ireland was opened, connecting Dublin with Kingstown, today known as Dun Laoghaire. Over the following century many more lines were built, and by 1920 Ireland had around 5600 kilometres (3450 miles) of railway track, encompassing almost every corner of the island. Today only about a third of these remain in use.

Belfast

City Hall, Belfast

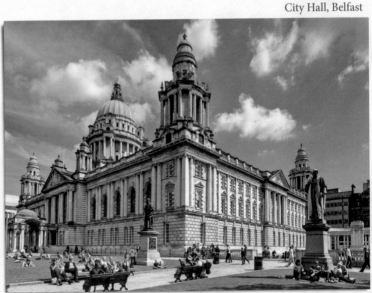

The linen industry was particularly significant in the North of Ireland. Belfast, strategically located on the western side of the Lough Foyle and at the mouth of the River Lagan, grew from a small market town to an important trade centre in the 18th century, supplanting Carrickfergus as the major port on the Ulster coast. In the 19th century it became a large industrial city, noted for the Harland and Wolff shipyard, which at its height employed over 35,000 workers. The most famous vessels to come out of the yard were the passenger liners Olympic (1911), Brittanic (1914) and the Titanic (1912), all built for the White Star Line. The story of the ill-fated Titanic is recounted in the impressive Titanic Belfast building, opened in 2012 on the site of the slipway where the ship was launched. Belfast's diverse Victorian architectural treasures include the immense City Hall (1906), the Grand Opera House (1895) and

Titanic Centre, Belfast

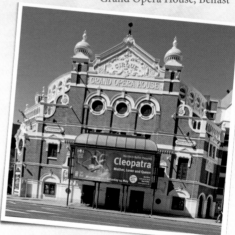
Grand Opera House, Belfast

R.M.S. Titanic

the luxurious Crown Liquor Saloon (1885), undoubtedly the most ornate 19th century pub in Ireland. The city suffered greatly during the 'Troubles' of the last three decades of the 20th century, but since the Good Friday Agreement of 1998 has re-established itself as a thriving and vibrant centre for business and the Arts.

Interior of the Crown Bar, Belfast City

Dublin

ublin also expanded greatly in the 18th century, becoming a great Georgian city. A succession of architectural masterpieces – starting with the Royal Hospital (Kilmainham) in the late 17th century – transformed the cramped and uncomfortable medieval town. Dublin Castle was rebuilt and its old Norman towers and walls demolished. Nearby, the City Hall was erected between 1769 and 1779. A little distance down the road, the Irish House of Parliament (now the Bank of Ireland) began construction in 1729. Trinity College – founded in 1589 by Queen Elizabeth – was extended and its impressive Library and Front Square laid down. Leinster House, a little distance to the south, was built in 1745 and now houses the Dail, or Irish parliament.

Trinity College, Dublin

everal important public buildings were built along the Liffey Quays, most famously the Four Courts and the Customs House, which many experts consider the finest building in Dublin. The Quays became a fashionable area, particularly around Capel Street. In addition to the many fine stone bridges which joined the older part of the city to the new streets on the northern side, the graceful cast-iron Halfpenny Bridge was opened in 1816. It has become a symbol of Dublin, along with the 'Liffey heads' that adorn the city's other bridges. Many architectural critics consider Dublin's terraces and squares of Georgian town houses to be her particular glory. They were built from the early 18th century onwards. The most fashionable areas were originally on the north side of the river

The Four Courts and River Liffey at night, Dublin City

The Ha'penny Bridge and River Liffey, Dublin City

Georgian Door, Dublin City

around Mountjoy Square, the first square of Georgian houses built in Dublin. In time, however, Merrion and Fitzwilliam Squares and their vicinity south of the river became more popular. Eventually the rows of magnificent Georgian terraces on the streets around O'Connell Street degenerated, and became the slum tenements depicted in the plays of Sean O'Casey.

Tall Ships Festival, Dublin City

The centre of modern Dublin – as befits any great city – is a mixture of several architectural styles. Many important Georgian buildings are still in everyday use, like the bullet-pocked G.P.O. building or the Rotunda – Europe's first maternity hospital. The Georgian core of the city has been supplemented by later Victorian and 20th century buildings. Some, like the beautiful Byzantine style University Church on St. Stephens Green built in 1855, are minor architectural masterpieces. Others date back to the Edwardian era and have a special place in the heart of Dublin's citizens. The traditional pubs of Dublin are of course rightfully famous, havens of Victorian grandeur where patrons sit at marble counters drinking Guinness Stout which has been brewed at the St. James 's Gate Brewery for over two hundred years.

The colourful Doors of Dublin

57

The twenty years between 1990 and 2010 witnessed an extraordinary transformation of Dublin. Semi-derelict areas around the Quays and Docklands were developed and rebuilt, whilst new features like the harp shaped Samuel Beckett Bridge across the River Liffey and the spectacular Aviva Stadium in Ballsbridge transformed the city's skyline. A new light rail system, the LUAS, was constructed at enormous cost to link the centre of the city with its outlying suburbs. The unprecedented Dublin building boom was paralleled in almost every town and city in Ireland.

Dublin's most enduring heritage, however, has been her long literary tradition. To a great extent this was laid down in the city's Protestant and Anglo-Irish past, although in the last century or so century more Catholic writers have come to the fore. The first great Dublin writer was Jonathan Swift (1667-1745), the Dean of St. Patrick's Cathedral. Although mainly remembered today for 'Gulliver's Travels', some of his best writing was contained in savage attacks on English misrule. Ireland's association with the theatre began in the later 18th century with the playwrights Goldsmith and Sheridan. At the end of the following century Oscar Wilde

Iconic entrance to the St. James's Gate Brewery, Dublin

and George Bernard Shaw continued this tradition in the English theatre. In Dublin the Abbey Theatre – co-founded by the great Irish poet W.B. Yeats – brought a new type of realistic drama to the stage – culminating in the plays of John Synge and Sean O'Casey. Later in the 20th century another Dubliner, Samuel Beckett, won the Nobel Prize for 'Waiting for Godot' and other modernist plays. To this day Irish theatre is amongst the most exciting in the world, with established and new dramatists regularly producing important works.

Irish Writers

Samuel Beckett
1906-1989

Oscar
1854-1900

W.B. Yeats
1865-1939

Brendan Behan
1923-1964

Brian O'Nolan
1911-1966

James Joyce
1882-1941

Oliver Goldsmith
1730-1774

J. M. Synge
1871-1909

Jonathan Swift
1667-1745

Sean O'Casey
1880-1964

Patrick Kavanagh
1904-1967

G. B. Shaw
1856-1950

Dublin's greatest writer was a novelist rather than a dramatist or poet. The foundations of James Joyce's reputation as one of the most important writers of the 20th century rest on his intimate knowledge of his native city. 'Portrait of the Artist as a Young Man', 'Ulysses' and his collection of short stories 'Dubliners' vibrate with the atmosphere of the city in Edwardian times and uniquely recreate that lost world. Although later writers like Brendan Behan and Brian O'Nolan have continued to place Dublin on the literary map, the worldwide perception of Dublin still owes much to Joyce's vision of the city.

The Long Room, Trinity College, Dublin

Modern Ireland

The Millennium year of 2000 marked a watershed in the history of Ireland. Since the country received its freedom from England in 1922 it had been rediscovering and re-inventing itself. The price of modernizing the country had included the unnecessary loss of much from the past that could not be replaced. Many

The Customs House, Dublin City

important Georgian country houses were destroyed or abandoned after Independence; over the following decades more of Ireland's architectural heritage - from cottage to Church to Castle and beyond - was depleted in the name of 'progress' and 'modernisation'. Yet, as the country became more self confident and aware of the value of its heritage, public opinion slowly turned to an appreciation of old buildings, whether the 'Big House' that was once despised as a symbol of an unpopular landlord or a simple lime washed cottage abandoned by its owner for a modern bungalow. At the same time Ireland - and particularly Dublin - became far more cosmopolitan, especially after the nation joined the European Union in 1972.

Temple Bar, Dublin

Molly Malone Statue, Dublin

I n the early 1990s a number of factors came together to trigger a cultural and economic explosion that made Ireland the envy of other European countries. These were the years of the so-called 'Celtic Tiger', when the country rapidly became immensely wealthy, and Irish cinema and music made their mark on the international stage. By the year 2000 Ireland seemed to be looking forward to a bright future of financial stability and full employment. In 2003 the economy faltered but seemed to revive again, buoyed up by the housing market and the activities of developers. This proved to be illusory, and in the aftermath of the worldwide financial crisis of 2008, the Irish building industry collapsed. The massive debts incurred by developers caused the bankruptcy of several leading banks and saddled the Irish Government with huge debts. The country was left with a massive financial hangover and economic problems that will take many years to resolve.

Samuel Beckett Bridge and the Convention Centre, Dublin Docklands

Grafton Street, Dublin

Most Irish people will agree that their homeland has started a new chapter in its long history. Despite the problems that followed the collapse of the Celtic Tiger economy, the Ireland of today is more tolerant and cosmopolitan than ever before. Cities and towns have become cleaner and more attractive, and there is a strong desire to preserve the island's natural and manmade heritage for future generations. The violent years of 'The Troubles' are slowly becoming a memory and relations between Northern Ireland and the Irish Republic have been stabilized. For visitors from abroad, both parts of the island, North and South, have much to offer, and the standards and selections of accommodations, restaurants and leisure activities are vastly higher than they once were. There is far more to see and do than in previous decades, and the natural beauty of the island remains largely unspoiled; few countries can boast such a diversity of landscape in so small an area. Above all, the Irish are still the friendliest people in Western Europe, and if they now consider themselves citizens of a modern European country, they are also the willing heirs to their own unique cultural and historical traditions.

JIM
LARKIN

1876-1947